FOREWO

David Nussbaum
Formerly CEO of WWF-UK

'Christian people should surely have been in the vanguard of the movement for environmental responsibility, because of our doctrines of creation and stewardship. Did God make the world? Does he sustain it? Has he committed its resources to our care? His personal concern for his own creation should be sufficient to inspire us to be equally concerned.'[1]

This essay sets out the biblical case underpinning that quote from theologian, practitioner, and co-founder of LICC, John Stott. Paul Kunert anchors this case in the life, death, resurrection, and return of Jesus – as did the Apostle Paul: 'Through [Christ Jesus] God was pleased to reconcile to himself all things, whether on earth or in heaven, making peace by the blood of the cross (Colossians 1:20)'.

Back in the 1990s when I worked in international development and humanitarian relief, I came across many Christians whose work to relieve poverty and suffering was an expression of their faith; indeed, many organisations were Christian in name and/or conviction, including World Vision, Christian Aid, and Tearfund. When I moved into conservation, however, there seemed to be far fewer Christians around, A Rocha being a notable exception. Two decades on, I'm thankful there is far greater recognition of the connections between the Christian faith and ecological issues, including climate change and biodiversity loss.

Paul Kunert explains how Jesus' death and resurrection extend beyond human salvation to encompass the reconciliation and restoration of the entire cosmos, which John 3:16 tells us

God loves so much that he sent Jesus, and which originally 'came into being through [Jesus]' (John 1:3). This essay underscores Christians' duty to care for the planet and its diverse forms of life, highlighting the urgent environmental crisis exacerbated by our self-interest-driven lifestyles. Recognising the inherent goodness of creation and God's plan for its renewal, culminating in the 'new earth' of Revelation 21:1, believers are called to steward the earth with reverence and selflessness. This stewardship, rooted in the image of God, intertwines with worship and service, shaping a holistic faith that integrates ecological concern with Christian discipleship.

The essay sets out how we humans have departed from God's intended order, degrading God's planet and exploiting nature, resulting in ecological breakdown. Embracing the gospel of Jesus as King is the solution: aligning our lives with God's mission for creation's flourishing, recognising Jesus' kingship over all creation, and participating in his mission of restoration. That entails lament and repentance, turning away from destructive habits, and embracing a life of faithful discipleship that prioritises the flourishing of the earth and the well-being of others. This is a transformative framework for addressing the crisis, both individually and in our churches. Living in harmony with God's purpose brings meaning and fulfilment to our actions.

I hope you too will find that Paul Kunert's essay brings insight, challenge, encouragement, and hope.

[1] *Foreword to 'Under the Bright Wings',*
Peter Harris (Regent College Publishing, 2000)

Unless otherwise indicated, Scripture quotations are
taken from the Holy Bible, New International Version
Anglicised. Copyright © 1979, 1984, 2011 Biblica. Used
by permission of Hodder & Stoughton Ltd, an Hachette
UK company. All rights reserved. 'NIV' is a registered
trademark of Biblica UK trademark number 1448790.

First published 2024

Design by Bori Ambrus
Printing by Haynes Mear

LICC Limited is a registered charity, No 286102, and
registered as a limited company in England and Wales,
No 01680265. Registered office address: St Peter's, Vere Street,
London, W1G 0DQ.

CONTENTS

—

Prologue

—

ON THE RIDGE

I stand on the ridge with my daughter, Bethany – storm on the horizon. 22 now, what does her future hold? For three years with the world's leading earth scientists, she has looked and she has seen. And now? She chooses not to look. Not to look, except, that is, when properly she has steeled her heart.

The wind already whipping at our faces, climate and ecological breakdown are upon us. Life ceases to teem, all creation groans, the poor are crushed. Yet week by week, in church gatherings, she and millions like her hear almost nothing about that breakdown, barring perhaps an occasional reminder to care for creation.

The main reason for that is not that we haven't taken the Genesis command to protect the earth seriously enough, nor even that we don't take Jesus' command to love our neighbour seriously enough. It's that we haven't understood and taken seriously enough the work of Jesus Christ on the cross for *all things*.

But for us who follow Jesus, the overriding reason to care deeply about the earth is that he does.

There are plenty of reasons to be concerned about what's happening to the earth. The breakdown threatens the intricate and beautiful world we love. It threatens our children's future, our vulnerable neighbours, and our own flourishing. So much so that he died to save it. But for us who follow Jesus, the overriding reason to care deeply about the earth is that he does.

This has deep implications for our lives. To see just how deep, we'll look squarely at the mess we're in and how we got here, at God's purpose for the world and for us, and then finally at how the news that Jesus is King is the answer to the breakdown. Because this news not only demands our obedience, but also restores to us our full humanity and leads us into the true worship of a life aligned with the maker of heaven and earth.

But first, the main thing.

RECONCILING ALL THINGS

God's redeeming purpose

> **'For God was pleased... through [Christ Jesus] to reconcile to himself all things, whether things on earth or things in heaven, by making peace through his blood, shed on the cross.'**
>
> –Colossians 1:19–20

Jesus died to reconcile all things to God, says Paul. Not just the planet, but all things, whether in earth or in heaven. The whole cosmos, we might say. Or the whole created order, everything with which the oceans teem and the earth and the skies are filled. He by whom, through whom, and for whom all things were made was by his blood shed on the cross reconciling all things. All things, including us humans. But not just us. All things.

We find the same in Paul's letter to the Ephesians. '[God] made known to us the mystery of his will according to his good pleasure, which he purposed in Christ, to be put into effect when the times reach their fulfilment – to bring unity to *all things* in heaven and on earth under Christ.' (Ephesians 1:9–10)

God's plan is to unite all things in Jesus Christ. Central to this plan, of course, is that we humans are redeemed and forgiven. We'll see the role we've been given as we go on. But for now, crucially, God's plan is to unite all things in Christ, put all things under his feet, and make him head over every thing (Ephesians 1:10, 22–23).

In case we're worried it's just Paul who thinks this way, we find the same in John's Gospel: 'Through him all things were made.' (John 1:3) Famously, he then goes on to say, 'God so loved [the cosmos] that he gave his one and only Son' (John 3:16). And, of course, Revelation closes with the great vision of renewal, a new heaven and a new earth, the holy city coming down from heaven to fill the whole earth. 'He who was seated on the throne said, "I am making everything new!"' (Revelation 21:5)

God's plan is global – cosmic – in scale. It's for the reconciling of (that is, making peace with) all things. It's for the uniting and renewing of all things. It's achieved through the blood of Jesus Christ shed on the cross. And centrestage is his redemption of humanity – we have an important part to play in God's mission. We'll come to that. Before we do, though, we must look squarely at the coming storm.

A STORM OF OUR OWN MAKING

—

Facing the breakdown

The planet, God's world, is in big trouble. Earth scientists are running out of words for urgency. 'Now or never.'[1] 'Final warning.'[2] 'Absolutely, gobsmackingly bananas.'[3] 'Crazy, off-the-charts records.'[4] 'We are damned fools.'[5]

As United Nations Secretary-General António Guterres put it, we're at 'Code red for humanity... the alarm bells are deafening, and the evidence is irrefutable: greenhouse gas emissions from fossil fuel burning and deforestation are choking our planet and putting billions of people at immediate risk.'[6] It's getting much hotter, fast. Pollution and destruction are pushing life everywhere over the edge, with terrible consequences for us, our neighbours, and the creatures around us, the birds of the air, the swarming creatures of the waters, the creeping things and wild animals of the earth.

Temperatures over the last five years are (on average) 1.2°C hotter now than in 1850–1900. In 2023, the average temperature was nearly 1.5°C hotter (yet another unwanted record), even reaching over 2°C for a couple of days in November.[7] Scientists expect it to take only a decade for these temperatures to become the norm.[8] On the course we're on, we'll reach a catastrophic 3°C hotter by the end of the century.

> 'WE LIVE OUR COMFORTABLE LIVES IN THE SHADOW OF A DISASTER OF OUR OWN MAKING. THE NATURAL WORLD IS FADING. THE EVIDENCE IS ALL AROUND. IT HAS HAPPENED DURING MY LIFETIME. I HAVE SEEN IT WITH MY OWN EYES. IF WE DO NOT TAKE ACTION NOW, IT WILL LEAD TO OUR DESTRUCTION.'[15]
>
> –David Attenborough

Earth scientists fear that beyond 1.5°C – the so-called 'safe level' – the earth is increasingly likely to reach tipping points – such as the melting of the Greenland and Antarctic ice sheets and permafrost, and the dieback of forests and rainforests. For example, as the ice sheets melt, less of the Sun's heat is reflected back into space, instead being absorbed by land and oceans, leading to further heating. The result: a heating cascade we can't control.[9]

Earth's fever is driven by our pollution. We dump carbon dioxide (from burning coal, oil, mostly as petrol and diesel in our cars, and gas, mostly for heating) and methane (from farming beef, lamb, and dairy) into the air, where it builds up and up and absorbs more and more of the Sun's heat.

Just like in the human body, every degree makes a huge difference.[10] Coral reefs – home to sharks and rays, barracuda, sun fish and angel fish, parrot fish and clown fish, and thousands of others – are dying. At 1.5°C hotter, 70–90% of coral reefs are lost, and at 2°C, more than 99%.[11] Amazon and Congo Basin rainforests gradually become dry savannah.[12] Closer to home, rising tem-peratures mean Atlantic Puffin breeding sites empty as heating oceans take their sand-eel prey too far from the colony.[13] It's the same for ecosystem after ecosystem. Innumerable species pushed to the edge and then – as it gets hotter – gone.

A hotter world isn't just bad news for the living ecosystems around us. It's bad news for us, too. First the poorest and most vulnerable, then everyone. Orbisa, bringing up her nine children in Ethiopia, has seen no rain for three years.[14] The riverbed dry, she now walks miles for water. In desperation she has slaughtered her livestock for food. She and her family must move to see if there is somewhere they can grow food or make a living.

As the Earth heats up, dry spells get longer and hotter and storms more intense, leading to more drought, famine, fire, and flood. We already see more frequent, more intense wildfires all over the world – in Australia,

Canada, California, Spain, Greece, the Arctic – and more powerful storms and severe floods from Carlisle to Karachi. The effects are felt most severely, however, in Africa and Asia, as lands that are home to hundreds of millions of people become gradually uninhabitable. This in turn drives increases in regional famines and global food instability, displacement and migration, people trafficking and modern-day slavery, burgeoning humanitarian crises, international tensions, and war.

A hotter and more volatile world is a growing driver of ecological breakdown. But, at least for now, it's not the biggest. It's how we produce our food that pushes ecosystems and habitats to the edge, along with the animal and plant species that thrive and flourish in them.

Rainforest is sacrificed to beef pasture and cattle feed (and timber and oil), mangrove forests to fish factories (and hotels), peatlands to game shooting (and compost and fuel) and hedgerows, meadows, ponds, streams, and rivers to industrial agriculture. Living soil becomes lifeless dirt.[16] Industrial fishing scours oceans all over the world, and seabed trawling rips up our kelp forests.

Oceans emptied of teeming life,[17] skies of soaring birds,[18] and lands of 'creeping things and wild animals'.[19] Hardly an ecosystem is not under threat from human activity. We make deserts, it seems, of all we touch.

It's not just that these ecosystems provide us with clean air and water, flood defences, soil sta-bility, and crop pollinators and help to keep the earth cool by absorbing greenhouse gases. It's that we also suffer the loss of the intricate beauty of the complex world around us.

The planet – we and all life on earth – is in big trouble. But that's not how it's supposed to be.

THERE IS NO PLANET B

—

God's purpose for the world

'God created the heavens and the earth... and God saw that it was good... God created [humankind]... and it was very good.'

–Genesis 1:1, 9, 27, 31

From Genesis to Revelation, we see that God's plan is the flourishing of the earth, not its destruction. God's first affirmation is that the earth is good. At the outset, even before God made humankind, everything he made – the land and the seas, vegetation, the fish of the sea, the birds of the air, and every living thing that moves upon the earth – was good.

Crawling leaf-cutter ant, squawking parrot, silent jaguar of the rainforest. Every handful of soil alive with billions of creatures. Ancient oak, home to a thousand species. Our island rocks, raucous with seabirds. The depths in which the whales sing. All of this is good, says the Lord God.

This wouldn't need elaboration if we Christians weren't so deeply influenced by the idea that matter doesn't really matter. It's an idea that comes from ancient Greek philosophy and Gnosticism, not from the Bible. And it plays out in our churches in non-biblical dreams of going to an ethereal heaven when we die, in worship disconnected from the rest of our lives, and the belief that God doesn't care that much what we do with the earth.

But God's message is that the world, this material world, is good.

And it's here to stay. God promises Noah – and every living creature – that never again will he destroy the earth (Genesis 9:8–11). God's promise *is* not that he will stop us destroying it, but is a commitment that he himself will not. Looks like the protestor's placard is right: there is no planet B.

But there is a *plan* B.

There is no planet B, but there is a *plan* B.

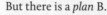

Then I saw 'a new heaven and a new earth... the river of the water of life, as clear as crystal, flowing from the throne of God and of the Lamb down the middle of the great street of the city. On each side of the river stood the tree of life ... And the leaves of the tree are for the healing of the nations.' (Revelation 21:1, 22:1–2)

God's purpose is not to do away with the earth, but to renew it. 'The consistent biblical hope from Genesis to Revelation is that God should do something with the earth so that we can once again dwell upon it in "rest", in Sabbath peace, with him. The Bible speaks predominantly of the need for God to come here, not of the wish for us to go somewhere else.'[20] (Christopher Wright, Global Ambassador and Ministry Director, Langham Partnership) Throughout the Old Testament, God gave his prophets visions of a time when all is made right. They're very earthly-minded visions. People will enjoy the fruits of their labours in peace and prosperity. Swords will be beaten into ploughshares. The wolf shall lie down with the lamb.

The New Testament picks up and expands these visions. In the great picture of the end in Revelation 21 and 22, we see the city of God, the holy of holies, filling the whole earth, rivers flowing out for the healing of the nations (Genesis 2, Ezekiel 47).

Even 2 Peter 3–13, which at first sight seems out of line with the otherwise consistent narrative arc of Scripture, on closer examination assures us that God is not betraying his promise to Noah. It is those same 'elemental spiritual forces' we are warned about in Colossians 2:8 that are to be dissolved with fire, not the entire earth.[21] The earth is purged, not destroyed, just as the church itself is tested by fire (1 Corinthians 3:10–15), but not destroyed.

Still, I've heard more than one evangelistic sermon along the lines of, 'The ship is sinking. Get in the lifeboat before it's too late.' But, bluntly, that's not the biblical picture. The consistent biblical picture is not of being rescued from here and taken somewhere else.

Biblically, there is no lifeboat. Just this ship. And the promise that, despite how it's all looking, it'll have a full refit and be as good as – no, better than – new. We *must* do away with the lifeboat picture and start talking about God's plan for the renewal of the ship.

God's plan is for the reconciling, uniting and renewing of all things

TO SERVE AS HE SERVES

God's purpose for humans

God has plans for the earth. And they hinge on his plans for humankind. It's absolutely clear from the opening chapters of Genesis that God has an important role and purpose for us.

Then God said, 'Let us make [humankind] in our image, in our likeness, so that they may rule over the fish in the sea and the birds in the sky, over the livestock and all the wild animals, and over all the creatures that move along the ground.' (Genesis 1:26)

We are, he says, to govern as he governs. 'Let us make humankind in our image, in our likeness.' Whatever else we might say about these words, the main picture is of humanity representing God on earth.[22] God is not represented on earth by an idol – an image or a likeness – in a temple. No, he is represented on earth by us. Humans are to represent him by governing with the same self-giving generosity by which he made the earth.

It's a glorious and beautiful vision for humanity. It's not just for powerful rulers, but for everyone. It's a vision of freedom – we are not slaves of the gods. And it's a vision of moral agency – we have responsibility. To govern as he governs is our purpose, our glory, our responsibility, and our joy.

We are the management team appointed by the owner, trustees of his foundation, tenants of his vineyard, crew of his ship. We are to lead, work, and govern in accordance with his self-giving purpose. Members of the whole community of creation to be sure, but first among equals, and with a special responsibility.

And if we want to know what it might look like to govern as he governs, we have a ready example. We look to Jesus Christ, the image of the invisible God (Colossians 1:15), the one who 'did not come to be served but to serve'. 'Whoever wants to be first must be slave of all.' (Mark 10:44–45) This is how God governs: in self-giving service.

This is reinforced in the second account of creation in Genesis 2:15: 'The lord God took the man and put him in the garden of Eden to work it and take care of it.'

The words in the original Hebrew are significant. 'Abad', translated here in the NIV as 'work', is nearly always translated elsewhere in the Bible as 'serve' and sometimes as 'worship'. Indeed, the Bible for Everyone translates it here as 'serve'.[23] The word carries the sense that in working the earth we also are to be serving it.

The word 'shamar', translated here in the NIV as 'take care of', is used elsewhere to speak of the priesthood's responsibility for the tabernacle (Numbers 31:30) It carries the senses of 'keep charge of', 'guard', and 'protect'.

What emerges from these passages is a beautiful picture of our worship, bound up with our work-as-service and our protection of the earth.

While God intends that we work and cultivate the land – and, by extension, create, design, and develop tools, goods and services that make for prosperity – it should always be in service. All of life and work is to be service to God, to one another, and the earth. And we are to protect the earth always, giving life, not destroying it. This is God's purpose for us. It is in this that we give glory to God. This is our worship.

We represent
God on earth.

We represent him
by governing with
the same self-giving
generosity we see
in his creation
of the earth.

BECOMING AS GODS

Rebellion is the root cause

It is a high purpose indeed. But one that we humans turn from almost before we've started. Desiring to become like God, we take and eat. Corruption, sin, and death mar God's world. Work becomes toil, brother murders brother, violence fills the earth. We inhabitants of the earth desire not God's glory, but our own. 'Shalom' – righteous peace and harmony with God, with one another, and with the earth – is broken. And so, the course is set for climate and ecological breakdown.

We humans – in our mutiny – have been bad for the world around us. It's not just a recent thing. From earliest humanity to today we've hunted animals to extinction: from prehistoric mega-fauna – woolly mammoths and nearly 150 others – to the Victorian tragedy of the flightless Great Auk, to the white rhino and the pangolin today. For thousands of years, for fuel and food – whether 'slash and burn' or rotational or more intensive farming – we've crushed the wild world around us. For as far back as we can see in history, we've treated the world around us as something to be exploited, not nurtured. With disastrous results for the rest of life on earth.

In the last 250 years, with the advent of the industrial revolution, something extraordinary has happened in human society. We've moved away from subsistence living to a much richer, more expansive, more materially prosperous way of life widespread in society. First in the UK, then the West, and now in most of the world, innovation, ingenuity, and technology have produced enormous improvements in child mortality, health, longevity, education, material prosperity, and quality of life, from modern dentistry to the magic of the washing machine.[24] Many more people are living richer lives.

It's not all bad for the world around us, either. The discovery of oil was the salvation of the whale. Gas heating replacing coal (which replaced wood) made the air in our cities cleaner than it's been for centuries and halved our CO_2 emissions. The invention of artificial fertiliser has served to feed the world, potentially on less land. And prosperity reverses population growth, reducing pressure on the world around us.

It may not be *all* bad for the world around us, but, as we've seen, it is pretty bad. Our emissions are driving climate breakdown, and industrial agriculture, effluent, waste, and climate breakdown are driving ecological breakdown. Our modern way of life is causing huge collateral damage. We may have been bad for the world around us ever since we left Eden, but today we're operating at such a scale that we're overwhelming it.

We live in very unusual times. Our prosperity means we have the luxury of choices our forebears perhaps didn't. It's within our power today to choose to live in a world of 10 billion (the global population expected by 2060) prospering people and flourishing wildlife. Or to choose not to. We have all the technology we need (though there's always room for improvement), and we know what we need to do.

We've known for a long time what's causing the breakdown, and we've known what's coming. At the Earth Summit in Rio de Janeiro way back in 1992, the nations agreed to tackle the big challenges of global heating and biodiversity loss. And yet at the time of writing, 28 rounds of negotiations later (28!), we've only just been able to say we need to 'transition away' from coal, oil, and gas. Half of all global emissions in history have occurred since the Rio Summit in 1992.

In Paris in 2015, the nations of the world came to an historic agreement to limit the global temperature rise to 2°C, and keep it as close to 1.5°C as possible. Since then, far from falling, annual emissions have gone up and up, and we're burning through ecosystems as fast as ever.

There are great gashes in the side of this ship. Yes, we've made some changes, plugged a few leaks, but nowhere near enough. Water's pouring in, the crew's still making the gashes wider and destroying the bilge pumps, and we have no bailer worth speaking about.

Since – obviously – it would be better to live in a prospering and flourishing world, how is it that, though we know the problem, and have all the solutions and technology we need, we have simply failed to act with the urgency and on the scale we need? How is it that we as individuals, corporations, and societies, are willing to allow such catastrophic collateral damage?

HEARING BUT NOT DOING

—

A sin, greed, and idolatry problem

Numerous books have been written by climate scientists on why we find it so hard to hear about and act on climate breakdown.[25] They say it's too abstract, or it's about people far away (or in the future), or it's about animals and plants, and so on. It may be that these reasons contribute to our inaction, but in truth we don't want to hear about it because it challenges one of the key tenets of our society: our freedom to pursue our own interest, whether that be individually, corporately, societally, or nationally. We are wilfully blind to the reality of the breakdown, for fear of what seeing may require of us.[26] We are willing to allow catastrophic collateral damage because preventing it would not be (or we fear it would not be) in our personal, corporate, or national interest.

We are wilfully blind to the reality of the breakdown, for fear of what it may require of us.

In scandal after corporate scandal, we see corporations and those who run them acting in the interests of the their own bottom line to the detriment of the world around them. Coca-Cola chooses to use plastic packaging even though its own report tells it the policy will create more plastic pollution, and then lobbies governments to prevent a bottle-returns policy in case it harms sales and profitability.[27] UK water companies have underinvested in sewage treatment to keep prices down and dividends up. Farmers – often responding to ill-thought-through incentive schemes – have torn out hedges, filled in ponds, and intensified the use of fertilisers and pesticides. And so we end up with plastic on our beaches, sewage in our oceans, deadly algae in our rivers, and our countryside stripped bare.

Oil and gas companies – though they were the first to know that their products cause climate breakdown – hid the truth and continue to lobby hard to keep it off the agenda.[28] They continue to drill for new reserves, even though they and we know that just burning the reserves we have today will push us past safe limits. Most now have given up on the pretence – if they bothered with it in the first place – of leading a transition to clean energy. It is in their interest to sell oil and gas for as long as they can. And so we end up with a rapidly heating world.

It's fairly easy to pick on faceless corporations, but the same goes for us too. Our self-interest as individuals may be more complex than purely financial. Purchases may signify status or identity. Accumulation may be about security. Choices may be for convenience or simply habitual. Or they may be purely financial. Or most likely some combination of the above.

What is it, for instance, that makes some of us react so strongly to the suggestion that we should eat a lot less beef? There is widespread agreement among climate scientists that doing so would have a far bigger impact than any other single change to the average UK diet. Eating less beef lowers greenhouse gas emissions enormously and frees up both grazing land and feedstock crop land for the restoration of ecosystems and the drawing down of carbon. It's a massive double win. It's also better for our health and our bank balance – so that's a quadruple win. Pretty much anyone could do this. But I've seen friends laugh out loud at the suggestion, go on to wax lyrical about the wonders of a match-day burger, or find ways to brand the vegan next to me a hypocrite.

Why do we have a similar reaction to the suggestion that we choose not to fly for holidays, that buying an SUV, yet another pair of jeans, or wear-once fashion is a bad idea, or that maybe we don't need this season's chic for our kitchen space? The alternatives – holidaying close to home, a smaller car, cycling or walking or taking the bus, eating less beef, buying less, upgrading less – needn't cost more.

Likewise, why do we react against suggestions on how we can get away from using petrol, diesel, and gas? Home heating is one of the biggest sources of emissions for most people. Insulating our houses or replacing our gas boilers with a heat pump are big wins. It might cost more than a gas boiler, although with the grants available at the time of writing, it needn't. But even if it did cost a bit more, how willing would we be to do it anyway, in the interests of others, as alignment with God's mission,

as worship, even? For some, even a bit more is simply unaffordable, but for many of us it's a matter of choice. And if it's a matter of choice, is financial self-interest our only measure? Really, the question is how would Jesus – who died to save the planet – have us respond?

There are lots of books out there on the drivers of consumer culture and our seemingly insatiable desire for more.[29] But however we look at the underlying reasons for not choosing the greener options, though they're available to many or most of us and though they make for the flourishing of the world around us and the good of our neighbour, it's self-interest that means we choose not to.

Finally, national self-interest also stops us acting. One of the main reasons why the UN COP process is so protracted is that it requires unanimity. Everyone has to agree with everything, including petrostates like Russia and Saudi Arabia. No wonder it's so difficult to agree we need to stop using oil and gas! Everyone is promoting their national self-interest. No one wants to run too far ahead in case others don't follow suit. But what if Saudi Arabia's position means that low-lying Tuvalu disappears beneath the waves? What if the UK's position means the same?

On greenhouse gases, we here in the UK have made some progress against our agreed target, but we still face a daunting challenge. At a little over 1% of annual global emissions, the UK might not be a big contributor now, but because we started the industrial revolution, we're still the fifth biggest in total. We're also the sixth biggest economy and one of the wealthiest countries in the world. Taking all that into account, the UK has set a target of a 68% reduction in emissions against 1990 levels by 2030.

As for progress, we've been doing well on getting our emissions down: we've nearly halved them since 1990.[30] But before we congratulate ourselves too quickly, although investing in wind and solar power have played their part, most of the reduction has been a happy by-product of things that were happening anyway: the result of shifting from coal to gas in our power plants, and shifting manufacturing to countries like China – more of an accounting trick than an actual reduction. We've achieved 47%, and so have 21% to go in the next six years. That's the same as reducing emissions from *today*'s level by 40% in the next six years, which is still a very tall order. No room for slacking off.

This progress we need to make as a nation isn't going to happen by the same happy coincidence. Some of the things we need to do are more or less underway (though likely to be late), like the transition towards a low carbon electricity grid and the shift towards electric vehicles. But others like home heating and diet changes are miles off, and few politicians seem to want to talk about them. It might cost us something. It certainly means we need to make some changes. Would we be willing to make them even if it might not be in the national interest? Often governments don't act because they believe people don't want change. But what if every Christian, every church community, called for change as an integral part of their mission, a way of serving and worshipping Jesus who died to make peace with all creation? Would we support or call for the Government to act?

In short, the reason we know but fail to act is that we put corporate, individual, and national self-interest above the flourishing of the earth and the good of our neighbour. Self ahead of God's glory. This is the toxic consequence of our mutiny in the garden. And it has led us inexorably to this time of climate and ecological breakdown.

The solutions our society offers us are partly an appeal to conscience ('make better consumer choices'), and partly an attempt to change the equation so that these choices are in our finanicial self-interest. We're stuck in a world of self-interest, financial calculus, status and identity, convenience and ease. And if we stay stuck there, the prognosis isn't good.

We put corporate, individual, and national self-interest above the good of the earth and our neighbour.

Self ahead of God's glory.

How far we have turned from our God-given servant-purpose! In mutiny, our rightly-ordered desires have become deeply disordered. Our God-given ingenuity may have brought us great prosperity but, combined with our God-rejecting mutiny, it brings us to the edge of the abyss. The prosperity of the modern world comes with the desolation of our common home. The breakdown is not so much a pollution-and-collateral-damage problem, but a self-interest problem – a sin, greed, and idolatry problem.

The history of humankind shows us that we don't have a coherent response to that. But God does.

THE MISSION OF THE KING

—

Making peace with all things

'The beginning of the [gospel] about Jesus the Messiah... Jesus went into Galilee, proclaiming the [gospel] of God. "The time has come," he said. "The kingdom of God has come near. Repent and believe the [gospel]."'

–Mark 1:1, 14–15

God's answer to the breakdown is the gospel. But, I've come to realise, in a much fuller way than we've traditionally understood it.

In our churches, we often use the word 'gospel' as shorthand for something else: perhaps a programme for social change or a set of propositions around sin, redemption, and eternal life. To the New Testament writers, though, the gospel is the news that Jesus, the Christ, the Anointed, has become King of the whole earth.[31] The rule of God, by way of the cross, resurrection, and ascension of Jesus, has begun.

'Gospel' is the word used for the announcement of a new king. The gospel of a new emperor in Rome would be proclaimed by messengers throughout the empire. The messenger of Isaiah brings the gospel: 'Your God reigns!' (Isaiah 52:7) When we hear the word 'gospel' we should expect to hear of a new king.

Using 'gospel' as the New Testament does, we might say that in the UK on 10 September 2022, the gospel of Charles III was proclaimed to the whole world: 'Charles III, by the grace of God, of the United Kingdom of Great Britain and Northern Ireland and of his other realms and territories King, Head of the Commonwealth, Defender of the Faith.'

The gospel of Jesus, the long-awaited Anointed, is that he has become king of the whole earth, bringing peace to all creation.

The announcement of the gospel – the news that Jesus is King – calls us to put our faith in him. In our culture, 'faith' is a word that's become muddled in all sorts of ways. To new atheists, faith means 'belief without evidence', Alice in Wonderland's six impossible things before breakfast. To government, society, and the media, faith is something only 'religious people' have, and so we hear about 'faith groups' and 'interfaith services' and so on. To some, 'faith' means the opposite of 'works'. But in the New Testament, faith is predominantly about commitment based on evidence. It's about belief, trust, faithfulness, allegiance, and loyalty.

There's a danger that, while we're rightly keen to emphasise we're saved by Christ's work alone, we speak only of belief and trust, forgetting Christ's call to faithfulness and loyalty. That is the

pitfall that Dietrich Bonhoeffer calls 'cheap grace'.[32] But Jesus says, 'Follow me'. And the apostle to the Christians in Rome says, 'Be transformed'. (Romans 12:2) The declaration that Jesus is King commands our allegiance. The news that he is King, in fact, is inseparable from his call to faithful discipleship.

And here we return to where we started. By his blood shed on the cross, Jesus was not only paying the price for the sins of the whole world but also making peace with all things. And in rising, he was not only showing that death is defeated but also that new creation is begun. The one who in crucifixion, resurrection, ascension, and outpoured Spirit has become King of all the earth has made peace with all things and is making the whole earth – in all its lush fruitfulness, its teeming, swarming, swooping, creeping splendour – new. Faithful discipleship, allegiance to this King, means living at peace with one another and with all things. Or to put it the other way around: careless (or not so careless) destruction of the earth runs in opposition to the work of Christ on the cross.

Though you could say it's simply a matter of obedience to the King (and you'd be right), it's also more than that. This is about our worship of the Creator-Redeemer God, and the pivotal role we hold in God's purpose for all creation. He is, in Christ, restoring us to our true humanity so the whole earth may be set free (Romans 8:20–21). What was broken by our mutiny, Jesus is re-making. He is reinstating the ship's crew.

In the beginning, we were to rule God's good earth as he rules it, so it could flourish and thrive. That's the purpose to which he's recalling us: to govern once more, not by self-interested domination and destruction, but in the same self-giving love as the Creator-Redeemer God. His purpose in Christ is nothing less than the restoration of our true humanity, responsibility, and moral agency, to forge us again into his likeness, to re-order our desires.

The flourishing of the whole earth is no sideshow for the creator God, but fundamental to his purpose and central to his mission. As central to the work of Christ on the cross as the reconciliation of you and me. It is this mission to which he calls us to align.

We who follow Jesus Christ are to be at the forefront of protecting the earth, not 'just' because God mandated us from the start to rule as he rules, to serve and protect it, nor 'just' because Jesus commands that we love our neighbour as ourselves, but *because it is central to the work of Jesus Christ on the cross* and to the mission into which he calls us. This is his purpose and in him, this is our purpose, our worship, and our joy.[33]

Christians are to be at the forefront of protecting the earth.

Because it is central to Jesus' work on the cross and our mission from him.

ALIGNING WITH HIS MISSION

The way of the King

'In this area as much as in any other, the key to our response lies in the recovery of the radical and comprehensive work of Christ on the cross and determined obedience to the mission of God in the world.' (Mark Greene, Mission Champion, LICC)

Living and working for the flourishing of the whole earth is integral to our discipleship, then, to our walking in the way of the King. For all of us, in the whole of life.

As in every aspect of our lives, Jesus doesn't set out a long list of rules, but calls us into a fundamental realignment of our whole selves toward God and others.

'Love the Lord your God with all your heart and with all your soul and with all your mind and with all your strength... Love your neighbour as yourself.' (Mark 12:30–31)

His commandment isn't arbitrary, but reflects the way the world really is. As we love God with our whole lives and love our neighbours as ourselves, we're living 'with the grain of the universe'.[34] In living out this command, we find what it means to be fully human again.

In every aspect of our lives – our governing and living and working and resting and playing and praying – we are to align ourselves with God's priorities, to serve as he serves, for the flourishing of the earth and the good of our neighbour. Because under the rule of God, the new creation, that's how the world really is.

By the working of the physics of carbon dioxide and global heating, the 'comfortable lives' we live impoverish the poorest and imperil the lives of our children. We are not to limit those whose good we seek, but, Jesus says, be a neighbour to the suffering, broken, and beaten. (Luke 10:36–37) In our interconnected, global world, this requires changes to how we live.

'WE MUST BE GLOBAL CHRISTIANS, WITH A GLOBAL VISION, BECAUSE OUR GOD IS A GLOBAL GOD.' [35]

–John Stott, theologian

All we do – working and resting, playing and praying – should align with God's priorities.

Serving as he serves, helping the earth and our fellow humans flourish.

Living our whole lives in line with God's redemptive mission isn't just our purpose – the apostle Paul says it's our true worship.

Living and working every day

As individuals, businesses, governments, and societies, we must ask what impact each action, commitment, and policy has on the flourishing of the living world and the good of our neighbour, not as an afterthought, but intrinsically, at the beginning.

It's here that the way of Jesus – his purpose, mission, and priorities – challenges our pursuit of self-interest and our habits of accumulation, identity, status, freedom, security, convenience, and ease. It's here in our work, in our daily lives, and in society that he calls for faithful allegiance. We're to live by self-giving service, not by self-interest.

'Therefore, I urge you, brothers and sisters, in view of God's mercy, to offer your bodies as a living sacrifice, holy and pleasing to God, which is your true and proper worship... be transformed...' (Romans 12:1–2)

Imagine if all our work – from farming to finance, teaching to tech, AI to zoology, boardroom to shop floor – was done with the flourishing of the earth and the good of our neighbour in mind. I might well ask, looking back over my own 25 years in the electricity industry, whether, if I'd had these at the forefront of my mind, I might have done some things differently. How might a farmer manage her land, or lobby government for change? Or a banker assess an investment in a new gas field? What opportunities might there be for us to speak up for truth and justice? When Coca-Cola was considering its plastic packaging, what might have been an intervention faithful to Jesus at the board meeting or during the project that preceded it? Or when Shell was considering investing in Canada's tar sands? Or at the oil companies whose scientists first confirmed the link to global heating so long ago?

What opportunities are there for us to 'make good work', to produce good goods and services that serve?[35] Or to mould the culture in our workplaces? Perhaps there are better ways to do what we do. Perhaps there are some things we just ought not to be doing. You'll know better than me how the Spirit is prompting you.

And imagine if all our buying and eating and using were defined not by self-interest, but by flourishing and good, seen as opportunities to minister grace and love. Jesus consistently calls us to turn away from money and possessions as sources of security and identity. Perhaps this used to feel like a 'victimless crime', but now we see the devastation our constant desire for more brings.

'Do not worry about your life, what you will eat or drink; or about your body, what you will wear... but seek first his kingdom and his [justice-righteousness].' (Matthew 6:25, 33)

Imagine if truly we didn't spend our time worrying about what we eat, drink, and wear, not to mention kitchens, curtains, cars, and long-haul holidays. Imagine if we sought first his rule and his justice-righteousness. How would we find ways to stand apart from our society's expansive, oil- and gas-powered way of life? Jesus travelled at three miles an hour, and never more than 200 miles from home. And he was the most human human, the true image of God. That says something about true flourishing. What if we said 'no' to 'more, further, faster'? Could we live by 'less, closer, slower' in the interest of others, as worship of God and for the flourishing of the earth? How might we find ways to grow in and model godly character in the way we live?

At its roots the breakdown is due to the pursuit of our own self-interest – our insatiable desire for more, for security, status, and identity – and the way of Jesus is the antidote to its poison. It's not a question of restraint (though we could with some of that) or of somehow making it in our self-interest to make good choices (though that wouldn't hurt), but of fundamentally reordering the way we see.

Being reinstated crew on God's ship – not a cruise ship, of course, but a working ship – is about all of life for all of us. We crew now in such a way as to be worthy of the Captain. We live our everyday lives in the power of the Spirit and in alignment with the God whose purpose and mission is the flourishing of the earth and the good of neighbour. This is not only our purpose – the apostle Paul says it is our true worship (Romans 12:1).

Speaking up for truth and justice

Living for the good of our neighbour and the flourishing of the earth in all of life must mean we do what we can in our homes, our communities and our places of work. But we need these changes across all of society, too.

Part of faithful whole-life discipleship is to speak up for justice, the good of our global neighbours, our brothers and sisters in vulnerable parts of the world, our children, and all the living world. They need us to call on our wider society to act more quickly for change. To call on governments for policies that get the balance right between good effective food production and the flourishing of the world around us, for example. Or for non-carbon electricity, localised town planning, energy efficient housebuilding, fisheries-friendly quotas and marine reserves, and beyond.

We have a vital and important role to play. Though sometimes we may feel powerless or overwhelmed, the reality is that Christian leaders – local and national – still do carry some moral, even perhaps electoral, weight in society, whether locally with their council or MP or in Parliament or at a demonstration. My local MP was renowned to be hard to reach on any issue, and he couldn't have been less interested in the 'green agenda'. But persistence by the pastor led him to meet with a delegation from our church community. In the meeting, he made the connections between the drivers of humanitarian crises, immigration, and conflict on the one hand (issues about which he was rightly concerned), and a heating world and the way we live on the other.

At a national level, the Church of England's partnership with the London School of Economics to measure companies' progress toward net zero emissions has been widely influential. Its recent decision to stop investing in oil and gas companies – because they are not doing what they need to to keep global heating under control – sent ripples through the investing world. It prompts others to ask whether they should be investing in those companies.

Church ministers' presence at a climate demonstration still makes the newspapers. Whether you agree or disagree with 'direct action' protests, the followers of Jesus I know who have taken that path are 'all-in', giving up their livelihood and even liberty for neighbour and the earth.[37] However the Spirit is be prompting you, may we all be all-in when it comes to our alignment with God's mission.

These are all ways we can, as part of following Jesus in all of life, call on society to become more aligned with the way of the King. But they're only partial. What our societies need, above all, is to come back into alignment with God, to have our desires reordered. And here we come to the final way in which we can act for the good of our neighbour and the flourishing of the earth.

Announcing
the gospel

The news that Jesus is King is God's answer to the climate and ecological breakdown. Not because he gives us a lifeboat. But because the captain reinstates his crew and reorientates us to his mission.

Now as much as at any time in human history, what we nee more than anything is the transformation that comes with this news. In him we have life in all its fullness, the promise of the renewal of all things, and a way of life to be lived.

In a society pursuing self-interest, and in nations whose negotiations have stalled at self-interest, how desperately we are in need of the servant King, who both holds out forgiveness and calls us to his servant way. It's essential that we announce the news that Jesus is King.

It is this news that gives our otherwise mundane actions meaning. Faced with the scale of the breakdown, the good and sensible actions commonly suggested to us by environmentalists – insulate your loft, cut down on meat and dairy, switch to an EV – can feel tokenistic. Without a wider framework of God's purposes for us and the world, the action does not feel adequate for the size of the problem.

Now as much as at any time in human history, more than anything, we need the transformation that comes with the news that Jesus is King.

But reorientating our lives to Jesus, through whom all things were made and who has made peace with all things – now *that* is an action commensurate with the scale of the breakdown. Turning to him in lament and repentance, turning from the way of life that leads to devastation, taking up his way, a complete reordering of our lives – *that* is a response worthy of the crisis. A life of faithful discipleship and alignment with God's mission imbues these otherwise apparently mundane acts with purpose and meaning – joy and peace, even.

Prayer before a meal

A simple way to regularly re-commit to living God's way in your daily life.

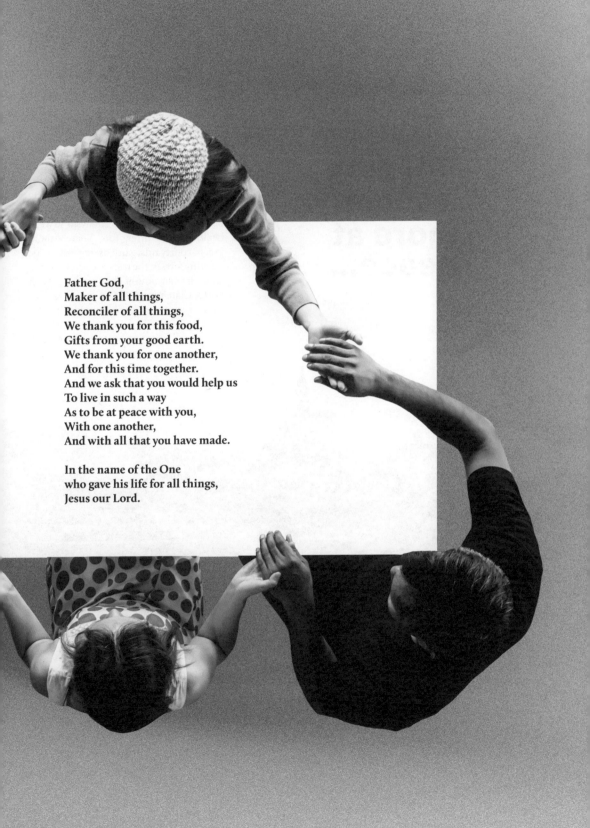

Father God,
Maker of all things,
Reconciler of all things,
We thank you for this food,
Gifts from your good earth.
We thank you for one another,
And for this time together.
And we ask that you would help us
To live in such a way
As to be at peace with you,
With one another,
And with all that you have made.

In the name of the One
who gave his life for all things,
Jesus our Lord.

Imagine a society more at peace...

In the city, the roar has become a hum. Pretty much everything is electric: heating, cars, trucks. The high street is busy, there are still vehicles zipping around, but the air is clear. There seem to be more people about these days, and we're healthier and fitter, too. There's more green: courtyards, gardens, revived rivers, and tiny forests, the trees a welcome shade when it's hot. And it does get hot, much hotter than it used to. Our buildings stay cool in summer, warm in winter: solar panels on every roof. Industry is thriving, and it's all about clean tech these days.

In the countryside, farmers have been partnering with ecologists for decades now. Ways of life have changed quite a bit. Rightly-grown food is properly valued, farmers make a decent living, and there's more work in our rural communities now than 20 years ago. Woodlands, heathlands, hedgerows, peatlands, wetlands, and waterways swarm with life. There're a lot fewer cattle, to be sure, but still some. Vast machines still do the harvesting, but not to the fields' very edge. The soil is recovering. Rivers run clear.

Nightingales sing in the blackthorn scrub. Beavers and salmon run in our rivers. Even lynx on former grouse moors. And our once near-empty oceans teem again. Inshore fishing communities thrive together with kelp forests and mussel beds. Deep sea catches, too, are higher now than they were two decades ago.

It's not so hard, is it, to be more at peace with the earth? And did I see my daughter there in the city, chatting with her kids, under the tree, in that café garden?

HIS PURPOSE, OUR PURPOSE

Three strategic steps

I am convinced the news that Jesus is King, and the whole-life discipleship he calls us to, are the answer to climate and ecological breakdown – either in bringing transformation to our society or in bringing hope as we witness faithfully to his purposes through dark times. But if we are to see that answer worked out in the world, we need to make a strategic shift in how we see ourselves and our purpose as God's church.

For the next few pages, I'm speaking primarily to church leaders, pastors, church councils, elders, and so on. If you're not in leadership, maybe you can take these suggestions to your leadership team. There are many steps we could take, small and large, easy and not-so-easy wins. But I'm not going to give you a long to-do list. To embed this core purpose of discipleship in your church community, I'm going to suggest three doable, strategic next steps.

Before that though, some good news: apart from some hard thinking as a church community at the beginning, this doesn't mean more meetings or another group to attend. Rather, it means a shift in how we see the purpose of the church, what we're aiming for, what we spend our time worrying about and how we talk about the gospel.

We need a shift in how we see the purpose of the church: what we're aiming for, what we worry about, and how we talk about the gospel.

And some more good news: this is likely to connect with younger people, many of whom have become disillusioned with church. They've known for years about the breakdown and seen the church for the most part practically oblivious to its devastation. Robust research shows that 9 out of 10 children, teenagers, and Gen Z-ers are concerned about climate change, 8 out of 10 think Christians should do something about it, but only 1 in 10 thinks the church is taking it seriously. And this is one of the key reasons why they're walking away from church or not taking us seriously enough even to explore what following Jesus might be about.[8] This isn't just a missional imperative, required by alignment with the mission of God, but also vital to the communication of the news that Jesus is King to those who either don't know the King of the cosmos or else think he doesn't care about what he's made.

Aligning with God's purpose

Here's the first next step. We've heard a lot about purpose and mission, both God's and ours. We need to take a long, hard look at how we talk about our purpose as Christian communities.

How we articulate our purpose feeds through into everything we do. If a power generation company says its purpose is 'to improve people's livelihoods and stimulate economic growth by providing clean, affordable, reliable electricity where it's most needed', it'll go about its business one way. If it says its purpose is to make as much money as possible for its shareholders, it will go about it in quite another.

What does your church's mission or purpose statement say? Does it say anything about protecting the earth or serving your neighbour? The church I'm part of in south London says we are 'ordinary people, following Jesus, for the good of the world'. That works pretty well. And behind that headline, we've declared a climate emergency, and committed to make sure every decision we take 'considers the impact of the climate crisis'. We have a long way to go as a community, but it's a really good start! So, step one: review your purpose statement with your church. Is it fit for – well – purpose?

Appointing champions

Second, flowing naturally from the first, come strategy and staff appointments. In the company I used to work for, we appointed people to deliver on our purpose and strategy. One of our key appointments was our Environmental and Social Director. He made sure we were all doing all our work in a way that helped communities and the world around us flourish. Our staff appointments and our allocations of responsibility reflect our priorities. It's popular in church communities to appoint a 'worship leader' or a director of music. That might be fine, but, if we're pressed for resources, wouldn't we do better to appoint a 'whole-life discipleship leader'? Wouldn't we do better to prioritise serving our neighbours and protecting the earth – our true spiritual worship – over a vibrant worship service? Dare we in fact bring our songs if we do not serve the poor and protect the earth (Isaiah 58, Amos 5)?

Wouldn't it make sense to have someone on the leadership team focused on whole-life discipleship? Not to do everything – this is about all of us in all of life – but to train, equip, and hold the team accountable for driving the change of focus in all areas of church and community life.

The redemption of the earth should be central to our mental map of the gospel.

It's not just present in passages about God's joy in creation or care for the poor.

Speaking about the gospel

Third, let's amend how we speak about and preach the gospel week by week. All too often, we revert to the mental shorthand of the 'lifeboat gospel'. We might – to pick an example from a recent church meeting near me – instinctively end a sermon on the first chapter of Matthew with a call to 'give your life to Jesus so that you can be saved'. Having opened up themes of the royal lineage of Jesus, God's intervention and new creation, wouldn't it be more fitting to the passage to call for faithfulness to King Jesus, for a life aligned with his priorities? To call for a life of discipleship made possible by Jesus' death and resurrection and the work of the Spirit, and possibly glance ahead to some key features of the way of Jesus?

This, then, is not a question of waiting for God's joy in creation or his passion for defence of the poor to pop up in a passage of Scripture – though they frequently do – but of the mental map we have of the gospel. When we're preaching on, say, Romans, 1 Corinthians, Ephesians, Colossians, or Revelation, it's how we point back to the beginning, God's good purposes for the flourishing of humanity and all the earth, to the restoration toward which he is working, and emphatically to the reconciling, peacemaking work of Christ on the cross for the whole earth.

And it's how we connect the inauguration of Jesus' rule, and his call to repentance, to seeking the flourishing of the earth and the good of our neighbour. Surely it's impossible, for example, to preach on Colossians without talking about God's mission to make peace with all things, the flourishing of the world around us, and his call to us to align with his mission.

The gospel is not about a lifeboat. At best, that's a half-gospel. Rather, it's about a captain, reinstated crew – a reinstatement only made possible by the cross and resurrection of Jesus – and a full refit to come. And this full biblical gospel both requires and empowers us to speak not *every* week, but generally week by week, into our self-interested world about God's calling for his people to follow his way of self-giving service, to defend the poor, love our neighbour, and serve and protect the earth. My experience is that this message resonates powerfully with those who otherwise seem to have little time for Jesus and church.

So, three strategic, doable first steps to embed this in our churches' life and work. Who can say how they might transform the vitality and growth of our church communities?

I wonder what might happen if we were to live out the servant-way of Jesus to the full. I wonder what such salt and light might mean for our society. I wonder what might happen if we were humbly and consistently to call for change.

And I wonder what might happen if we were to proclaim – and to equip our people to proclaim in their everyday lives – the news that Jesus is King: the Jesus through whom all things were made, who was by his blood shed on the cross making peace with all things.

Who can say how transformed church communities might transform the communities they serve and wider society? And perhaps in God's mercy, the flourishing of the earth and neighbour? Or perhaps we simply are called to faithful witness, to a life of faithful discipleship in a deeply troubled and disordered world. Who can say? Either way, we have a unique basis for action.

And we have too a unique ground for hope.

HOPE ACTUALLY

Facing the storm with confidence

Genuine hope is hard to sustain in climate activist circles and even among climate negotiators. But there's plenty of anger, fury, rage, and frustration. Plenty of grief, despair, resignation, anxiety, and fear, even. But we have a hope grounded on the promise that one day God will bring to completion the work of reconciliation accomplished in the cross of Christ. All will be put right, the dead in Christ will be raised, and the good, just, peaceable, servant rule of God will at last be uncontested.

So we hear the angel: 'The time has come for... destroying those who destroy the earth' (Revelation 11:18). The destroyers of the earth *will* be destroyed. Death, mourning, crying, pain will be no more. *This* is our hope in Jesus Christ.

It is this hope that means we can look calamity in the face and not turn away. We don't deny the storm, nor fall into despair, nor conjure naïve optimism, but act in hope that all will be made new.

The promise of renewal also gives rise to a second hope. The hope that as we live and act in accordance with the way of Jesus, in the power of the Spirit, God may yet bring change beyond what we can imagine. If the Christian community is God's means of change – God's means for the blessing of the nations – and we live into our God-given purpose and role, God's blessing may yet be poured out on all the earth.

We have solid grounds for hope, and we *experience* it as we act. Hope rises as we live with the grain of God's universe. As we align with the mission of God, we are drawn into the life of God, and hope rises.

In this time of breakdown, we who follow the way of Jesus have something that only we can say.

We have a response that is rooted neither in self-interest nor the success of international negotiations, neither overwhelmed nor naively optimistic, neither driven by guilt nor fear nor even efficacy, but rooted rather in God's purpose for us, all humanity, and the whole earth. It is a response rooted in and compelled by the declaration that Jesus, through whom *all things* were made and by whom *all things* are reconciled to God, is King. It is a matter of faithful discipleship and true worship, alignment of all that we are with the mission of God.

The rightful King of all the earth has taken up his throne. The maker of all things has paid the price for our mutiny, liberated all things, reconciled and made peace with all things, and begun his rule. And, when all things have been put under his feet, he will finally intervene once more to make all things new, the great garden-city of God filling all the earth.

He calls us from the ways that lead to destruction to the way of Jesus Christ. Turning to him we joyously receive the gift of life, the promise of resurrection. We receive his indwelling Spirit that we may walk in his way of life, filled with his love, aligned in every respect with his purposes, seeking the good of our neighbour as much as our own, pursuing justice, making peace, and serving and keeping the earth.

Reinstated to our purpose, our moral agency recovered, how then shall we be found on the day of the returning King?

Say among the nations
'The Lord is king!
The world is firmly established;
it shall never be moved.
He will judge the peoples with equity.'

Let the heavens be glad,
and let the earth rejoice;
let the sea roar, and all that fills it;
let the field exult,
and everything in it.

Then shall all the trees of the forest
sing for joy before the Lord;
for he is coming, for he is coming
to judge the earth.

–Psalm 96:10–13, NRSV

Epilogue
—

ON THE
RIDGE

Standing on this ridge with my daughter, I can't say I know what the future holds. It may be that as we live and act and speak, God brings about a great change of direction. Or it may be that international negotiations fail and we breach 2°C, 3°C, or worse. It may be that we humans make deserts of the teeming glories of God's world.

But let it not be because we, his people, have not lived the way of the King. Let it not be because we have not called for change. And let it not be that we've failed to proclaim the kingship of the one who created all things and gave his life so all things might be renewed.

And so, we pray.

We lift our voices in petitioning our Father, we call for the rule of Christ in our Christian community and in our society, we call on God for restored purpose and agency, for peace with one another and with all the earth, for alignment to God of every part of our being, and for the flourishing of the earth and the good of neighbour.

We pray:

May we have
peace with the earth
 and justice for the poor,
deep change and great turning,
and the shalom of the rule of Jesus.

About the author

Born and bred in the UK, Paul has been working in Africa's electricity sector for the last 25 years in various senior leadership roles, developing, financing, building, and managing major power plants in countries all over the continent. He is a chartered accountant and has a degree in economics and politics. He is married to Tara and they have three grown-up children.

For a long time – far too long – he'd seen 'climate change' as a secondary concern, not something very high on God's to-do list. Either world leaders were on top of it, or it wasn't that big of an issue anyway. Or worse still, maybe God wasn't that bothered.

When the truth about climate and ecological breakdown – and God's purpose for his creation and the full extent of the work of Christ on the cross – finally hit home, he realised he couldn't have been more wrong.

End notes

[1]Jim Skea, Co-Chair of IPCC Working Group III, 'UN Climate Report: It's "now or never" to limit global warming to 1.5 degrees' (UN press release, 4 April 2022)

[2]Kaisa Kosonen, climate expert, Greenpeace International, 'Scientists deliver "final warning" on climate crisis: act now or it's too late' (*The Guardian*, 20 March 2023)

[3]Zeke Hausfather, research scientist, Berkely Earth, X post (3 October 2023)

[4]Prof Matthew England, University of New South Wales, '"Off the charts records": Has humanity finally broken the climate?' (*The Guardian*, 28 August 2023)

[5]James Hansen, former Nasa climate scientist, '"We are damned fools": scientist who sounded climate alarm in 80s warns of worse to come' (The Guardian, 19 July 2023)

[6]'Secretary-General Calls Latest IPCC Climate Report "Code Red for Humanity", Stressing "Irrefutable" Evidence of Human Influence' (UN press release, 9 August 2021)

[7]*The 2023 Annual Climate Summary* (Copernicus C3S, 2024)

[8]'We've "lost" 19 years in the battle against global warming since the Paris Agreement' (Copernicus C3S, 12 December 2023)

[9]Timothy M Lenton, *Global Tipping Points – Summary Report* (Global Systems Institute, University of Exeter, 2023), p5

[10]Katharine Hayhoe, *Saving Us* (Atria/One Signal, 2021)

[11]*Climate Change 2023 Synthesis Report – Summary for Policymakers* (IPCC, 2023), p17

[12]Timothy Lenton, section 1.3.2.1

[13]Adam Nicholson, *The Seabird's Cry* (Harper Collins, 2018), pp341–347

[14]Jane Boswell, *Living in fear: Ethiopia and the climate crisis* (Tearfund article, 15 October 2020)

[15]David Attenborough, 'A sixth mass extinction by 2100: Sir David Attenborough reveals how those born today could witness these scenarios unless we save the planet' (*The Mail On Sunday*, 14 September 2020)

[16]James Rebanks, *English Pastoral* (Penguin, 2021), pp142–145

[17]Charles Clover, *Rewilding the Sea: How to Save Our Oceans* (Witness Books, 2022), pp183–197

[18]Benedict MacDonald, *Rebirding: Restoring Britain's Wildlife* (Pelagic Publishing, 2020), pp1–31

[19]Living Planet Index, World (Our World in Data, 1 September 2023)

[20]Christopher J H Wright, *Old Testament Ethics for the People of God* (IVP, 2010)

[21]Christopher J H Wright, *The Great Story and the Great Commission* (Baker Academic, 2023)

[22]J Richard Middleton, *The Liberating Image: The Imago Dei in Genesis 1* (Brazos Press, 2005)

[23]John Goldingay and Tom Wright, *The Bible for Everyone* (SPCK, 2018)

[24]Hans Rosling, 'The Magic Washing Machine' (TED Talk, December 2010) and *Factfulness* (Sceptre, 2018)

[25]George Marshall, *Don't Even Think About It* (Bloomsbury, 2015) and Katharine Hayhoe, *Saving Us* (Atria/One Signal, 2021)

[26]Margaret Heffernan, *Wilful Blindness* (Simon & Schuster, 2011)

[27]Michael E Mann, *The New Climate War* (Scribe, 2021), pp52–60

[28]Ibid.

[29]For example, Ruth Valerio, *Just Living* (Hodder Faith, 2020)

[30]Hannah Ritchie, Pablo Rosado, and Max Roser, 'Per capita, national, historical: how do countries compare on CO2 metrics?' (Our World in Data, 26 September 2023)

[31]Matthew W Bates, *The Gospel Precisely* (Renew.org, 2021) and Tom Wright, *How God Became King* (SPCK, 2012)

[32]Dietrich Bonhoeffer, *The Cost of Discipleship – Repackaged Edition* (SCM Press, 2024)

[33]Christopher J H Wright (2023), chapters 7–8

[34]Stanley Hauerwas, *With the Grain of the Universe* (Baker Academic, reprinted 2013)

[35]John Stott, 'The Living God Is a Missionary God', quoted in James E Berney (ed.), *You Can Tell the World* (InterVarsity, 1979), p9

[36]See LICC's 6Ms of Fruitfulness framework for ideas (licc.org.uk/6ms)

[37]Sue Parfitt, *Bodies on the Line* (Labora Press, 2023)

[38]Burning *Down the House* (Tearfund report, 2023)

ABOUT LICC
—

Imagine if every Christian lived their life as Jesus would.

It would transform the people and places around them. It would change their organisations, communities, and societies. And it would change the world – ecologically, socially, economically, politically – as God works in and through his people, right where they are.

But most Christians tell us they have neither the vision nor the tools for the task. That's where LICC comes in. We're working to catalyse a movement that empowers Christians to live as disciples of Jesus in daily life.

We're here to help people know God more deeply and bring his wisdom, grace, and truth to the things they do – at work, at college, and at home; in the pub, the shops, and the gym; on social media, in the office, and out with friends.

We work with individuals, church leaders, and those who train them, partnering with organisations and networks across the denominations. We delve into the Bible, think hard about contemporary culture, and listen carefully to God's people, exploring the challenges and opportunities they face.

What we do comes out of what we learn. Resources, events, training, articles, books, films, stories, and more – all designed to encourage whole-life discipleship.

Jesus calls people into a movement of hope that will bring life to every human being and the entire planet. Today, the need for disciples living out that hope day by day is as great as ever. We're working to engage over a million UK Christians with this whole-life vision.

—

@liccltd 🅾 𝕏 **f** **in**
Discover more at licc.org.uk

MORE FROM LICC

Fruitfulness on the Frontline

This small group discussion series and book will inspire you to join in God's world-redeeming work in your everyday life, walking through six key ways we can all make a difference with him – wherever we are, whatever we do.

licc.org.uk/fruitfulness

Vital Signs

Designed for church leaders of all kinds, this simple online assessment with accompanying book, videos, and articles will reveal how you're doing at making whole-life disciples – and help you plan next steps for your church.

licc.org.uk/vitalsigns

The Gateway Seven Bible studies

Each of these seven Bible studies explores a different genre, helping you read law, prophecy, narrative, letters, wisdom, apocalyptic, and gospel books with fresh eyes – and discover the whole-life implications of Scripture.

licc.org.uk/gateway-seven

SHARE THIS ESSAY

—

You've read it – what now?

Share it around

Jesus Died to Save the Planet is available free as a blog and a downloadable PDF, as well as in hard copy. Who could you give it to? Share the link, send the PDF, or buy multiple paper copies to give away. The more people it reaches, the bigger the impact we can have for God's glory and the good of the world. Find it all at licc.org.uk/planet

Recommend it to your church leadership team

If we're going to turn the tide on climate breakdown, it's crucial our churches equip us as whole-life disciples, seeking to do every part of life with and for Jesus. Share this essay with your church's leaders and invite them to read and respond – how could your programme, preaching, groups, and more equip people to live that way?

Discuss it with a group

Get together with others from your church and chat about how you can respond to the message that Jesus died to save the planet – in your Monday to Saturday lives and as a church community.

licc.org.uk/planet

'There is no planet B. But there is hope for God's world. Because Jesus died to save the planet. Paul Kunert argues compellingly that creation care is gospel witness. Essential reading for Christians and church leaders on the most pressing issue of our time. Be inspired. And take action.'

Revd Dr Joanthan Rowe

Rector, St Paul's & St Matthew's, Winchester

'Paul Kunert has packed lots of rich theology, knowledge, and wisdom into these short pages. Writing with honesty and clarity he draws clear lines between human rebellion from God and our treatment of his planet. What makes the book stand out is Paul's argument from the redemptive purpose of Jesus' death and resurrection to our creation care as Jesus' loyal followers. Hugely stimulating and warmly recommended for every Christian to read and pray over, Paul's thinking has helped me and will certainly help our church to grow in faithful allegiance to Christ as we care for this planet.'

Andrew Towner

Vicar, Houghton and Kingmoor, Carlisle; Chair, Carlisle Diocesan Board of Education; Chair, Church Society Council

'I have found Paul's booklet to be lots of things: a helpful gospel corrective; a concise overview of the current climate crisis; and how allegiance to King Jesus demands we live a different way. I've read it, re-read it, am wrestling with its practical outworkings into the life of our church, and I am making sure everyone at our church gets a copy!'

Simon Lang

Neighbourhood Church, Beckenham

'A sobering must-read read for all Christians today. There are some hard facts to face about climate breakdown and biodiversity loss, yet you will be left with a clear road map and invitation towards faithful Christian living in the face of this. Theological, fact-filled, persuasive, and practical reading that leads to a place of true hope.'

Andy Atkins

CEO, A Rocha

More endorsements inside front cover

The gospel isn't just good news for humanity. It's good news for the whole planet.

The breakdown of the earth's climate and ecology is deeply rooted in human sin. Yet all too often we treat protecting nature as a fringe issue – a specialist topic that some Christians care about, not an essential part of the church's mission.

But Jesus died and rose to reconcile and renew all things – people, animals, plants, and the earth itself. That means that helping creation flourish is central to following him. We must live our whole lives in line with God's mission: for his glory and the good of the entire world.

Clear-eyed, biblical, and hopeful, this essay will help you rediscover God's good purposes for his world, achieved through Jesus' work on the cross. And in response, it will inspire you to Christlike action.

'There is a prophetic, Jeremiah-like urgency to this small book, calling the church to wake up and get serious about this issue. But, also like Jeremiah, Paul Kunert calls for repentance and holds out hope.'

Chris Wright
Global Ambassador, Langham Partnership

licc.

@liccltd 🅾 𝕏 f in